PIANO

Adventures® *by Nancy and Randall Faber*

_____ is sightreading this book!

(your name)

Production Coordinator: Jon Ophoff
Cover and Illustrations: Terpstra Design, San Francisco

ISBN 978-1-61677-672-5
Copyright © 2015 Dovetree Productions, Inc.
c/o FABER PIANO ADVENTURES, 3042 Creek Dr., Ann Arbor, MI 48108.
International Copyright Secured. All Rights Reserved. Printed in U.S.A.
WARNING: The music, text, design, and graphics in this publication are protected
by copyright law. Any duplication is an infringement of U.S. copyright law.

CHART YOUR PROGRESS

Sightreading for Lesson Book 3B, pp. 8–9
Energico 6–9

DAY 1   DAY 2   DAY 3   DAY 4   DAY 5

Sightreading for Lesson Book 3B, pp. 27–29
Legend of Madrid 32–35

DAY 1   DAY 2   DAY 3   DAY 4   DAY 5

Sightreading for Lesson Book 3B, pp. 10–11
Fiesta España 10–13

DAY 1   DAY 2   DAY 3   DAY 4   DAY 5

Sightreading for Lesson Book 3B, pp. 32–33
Phantom of the Keys 36–39

DAY 1   DAY 2   DAY 3   DAY 4   DAY 5

Sightreading for Lesson Book 3B, pp. 16–17
Sea Chantey 14–19

DAY 1   DAY 2   DAY 3   DAY 4   DAY 5

Sightreading for Lesson Book 3B, pp. 34–35
Humoresque 40–45

DAY 1   DAY 2   DAY 3   DAY 4   DAY 5

Sightreading for Lesson Book 3B, pp. 18–19
Rage Over a Lost Penny 20–23

DAY 1   DAY 2   DAY 3   DAY 4   DAY 5

Sightreading for Lesson Book 3B, pp. 36–37
The Bear 46–49

DAY 1   DAY 2   DAY 3   DAY 4   DAY 5

Sightreading for Lesson Book 3B, pp. 20–21
Finale 24–27

DAY 1   DAY 2   DAY 3   DAY 4   DAY 5

Sightreading for Lesson Book 3B, pp. 42–43
Liebestraum 50–55

DAY 1   DAY 2   DAY 3   DAY 4   DAY 5

Sightreading for Lesson Book 3B, p. 26
Baroque Dance 28–31

DAY 1   DAY 2   DAY 3   DAY 4   DAY 5

Sightreading for Lesson Book 3B, p. 45
Barrelhouse Blues 56–59

DAY 1   DAY 2   DAY 3   DAY 4   DAY 5

Sightreading for Lesson Book 3B, pp. 46–47
**The Piano Playin'
Chocolate Eater's Blues**............. 60–63

☐ ☐ ☐ ☐ ☐
DAY 1   DAY 2   DAY 3   DAY 4   DAY 5

Sightreading for Lesson Book 3B, pp. 56–57
Adagio and Allegro...................... 80–85

☐ ☐ ☐ ☐ ☐
DAY 1   DAY 2   DAY 3   DAY 4   DAY 5

Sightreading for Lesson Book 3B, p. 50
Gavotte 64–67

☐ ☐ ☐ ☐ ☐
DAY 1   DAY 2   DAY 3   DAY 4   DAY 5

Sightreading for Lesson Book 3B, pp. 58–59
Gypsy Camp................................. 86–89

☐ ☐ ☐ ☐ ☐
DAY 1   DAY 2   DAY 3   DAY 4   DAY 5

Sightreading for Lesson Book 3B, p. 51
The Return.................................... 68–71

☐ ☐ ☐ ☐ ☐
DAY 1   DAY 2   DAY 3   DAY 4   DAY 5

Sightreading for Lesson Book 3B, pp. 60–63
Pachelbel Canon........................... 90–95

☐ ☐ ☐ ☐ ☐
DAY 1   DAY 2   DAY 3   DAY 4   DAY 5

Certificate of Completion 96

Sightreading for Lesson Book 3B, pp. 52–53
Swing Low, Sweet Chariot 72–75

☐ ☐ ☐ ☐ ☐
DAY 1   DAY 2   DAY 3   DAY 4   DAY 5

Sightreading for Lesson Book 3B, p. 55
Rhythm Puzzle 76–79

☐ ☐ ☐ ☐ ☐
DAY 1   DAY 2   DAY 3   DAY 4   DAY 5

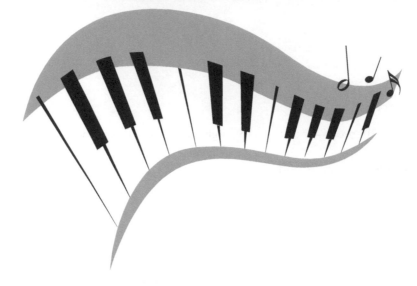

SIGHTREADING SKILL

Sightreading skill is a powerful asset for the developing pianist. It makes every step of music-making easier. With the right tools and a little effort, sightreading skill can be developed to great benefit.

This book builds confident, early-intermediate sightreaders in these ways:

1. Facile recognition of **note names**, including **ledger line notes**.

2. Recognition of the **major** or **minor key** with an understanding of its tonality; tonic, dominant, leading tone, and primary chords I-IV-V7 (or i-iv-V7).

3. Perception of common **rhythmic** and **melodic note patterns**.

Music reading involves more than a sequence of note names. The sightreader tracks *horizontally* and *vertically*, observing melodic and harmonic intervals, chords, rhythmic and melodic motives, dynamics, and accompaniment patterns that make up the context of the music.

This decoding skill requires repetition within familiar musical frameworks. In other words, pattern recognition develops by seeing a lot of the same patterns. Accordingly, this book presents **musical variations** to sharpen perception of the *new* against a backdrop of the *familiar*. More than any other instrumentalist, the pianist must group notes into patterns for musical understanding.

In the Level 3B Sightreading Book, these musical variations are drawn from the music introduced in the 3B Lesson Book—Beethoven, Dvořák, Rebikov, Liszt, J.C. Bach, and Pachelbel—as well as traditional folk songs and Faber originals.

The book features the keys of Am, Em, and Dm, with their scales and primary chords, along with sixteenth notes and chord inversions.

Get ready for a 3B Sightreading Adventure!

How to Use

This book is organized into sets of 5 exercises for 5 days of practice. Each set provides variations on a piece from the Piano Adventures® Level 3B Lesson Book. Play one exercise a day, completing one set per week.

Though the student is not required to repeatedly "practice" the sightreading exercise, each should be repeated as indicated by the repeat sign. For an extra workout, play each of the previous exercises in the set before playing the new exercise of the day.

Curiosity and Fun

The "Don't Practice This!" motto is a bold statement which has an obvious psychological impact. It reminds us that sightreading is indeed the first time through and it reminds us to keep the activity fun.

Level of Difficulty

It is most beneficial to sightread at the appropriate level of difficulty. By setting a slow, steady tempo, the student should be able to play the majority of the notes, especially on the repetition. This Piano Adventures® Sightreading Book is carefully written to provide an appropriate challenge for the Level 3B student.

Marking Progress

In previous levels, students were encouraged to draw a large **X** over each completed exercise. Due to the higher level of the student, this is now optional.

Some students may exclaim about the thickness of the book. They soon are rewarded to find how fast they can move through it. Indeed, with confidence increasing, the student can take pride in moving to completion of this very large book ... and do so with a crescendo of achievement.

Instructions to the Student

1. **Always scan the music before playing.**
   This strategy helps you "take in" the music you will be sightreading.
   You will get better and faster at "scanning" with experience.

2. **Scan the basics first.**

   - What is the key? Major or minor?

   - What is the time signature?

   - What measures look difficult? Mentally hear them before playing.
     You may wish to tap the rhythm lightly in your lap.

   - Now look for patterns. Are there any measures that repeat? How many?

   - Can you spot I, IV, or V7 chords?

   - Scan for scale passages and thumb-crossings. Any hand shifts?

   - Now scan for dynamics, sharps, flats, naturals, and rests.

3. **Count-off the tempo.**

   - Set a slow, steady tempo of two measures. Keep your eyes moving ahead as you play! Repeat the exercise.

   - You may wish to put a big X through the music to show completion.

DAY 1: Energico
Key of A Minor

Mentally hear the rhythm of measures 1-2 before playing. Silently finger the L.H. chords.

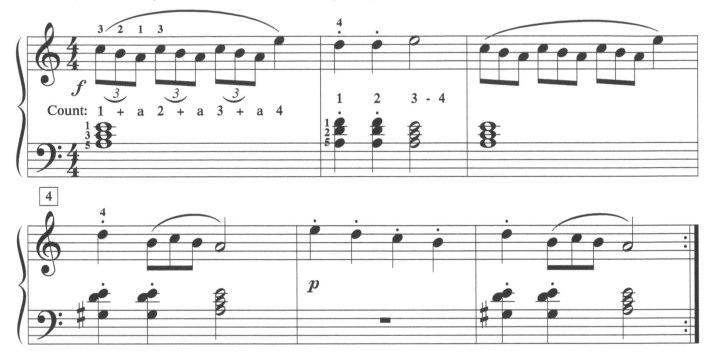

DAY 2: Energico
Key of A Minor

Mentally hear the rhythm of measure 1 before playing.

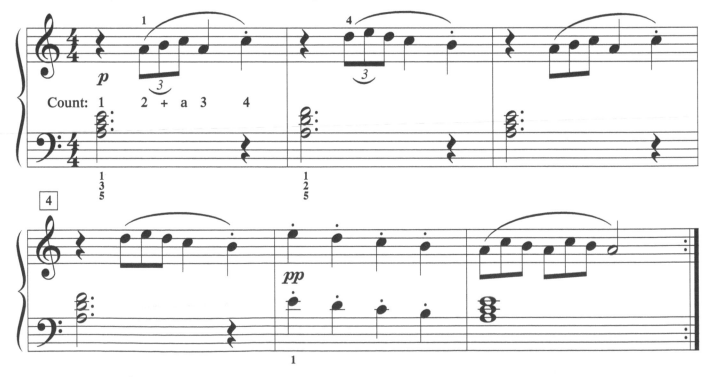

DAY 3: Energico

Key of _____ Major/Minor (circle)

Mentally hear the rhythm of measure 1 before playing.

DON'T
PRACTICE
THIS!

Count: 1   2 + a 3 - 4

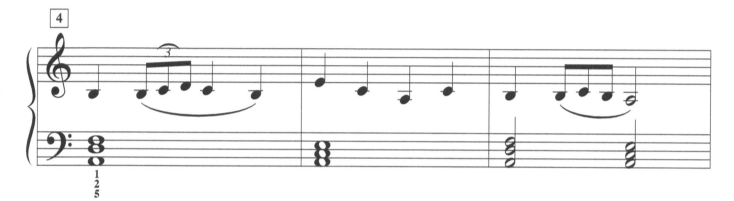

Circle all the A minor blocked or broken chords. Hint: There are three.

DAY 4: Energico

Key of _____ Major/Minor
(for L.H. alone)

Mentally hear the rhythm of measure 4 before playing.
Use this beat to set the opening tempo.

Write 1 2 3 4 under the correct counts.

SIGHTREADING

DAY 5: Energico

Key of _____ Major/Minor

Scan the music. Mentally hear the rhythm of measure 1 before playing.
Silently finger measures 9-11 before playing.

Count: 1   2 + a 3 + a 4

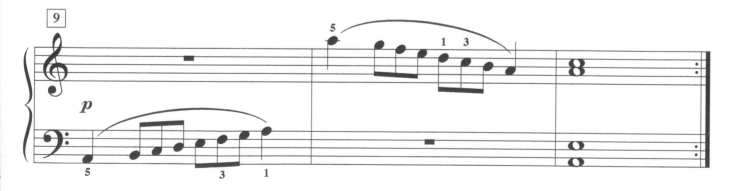

9

DAY 1: Fiesta España
Key of _____ Major/Minor

DON'T PRACTICE THIS!

Scan the music. Do you see a pattern? Notice the hand shifts going down the keyboard.
Count the opening measure before sightreading.

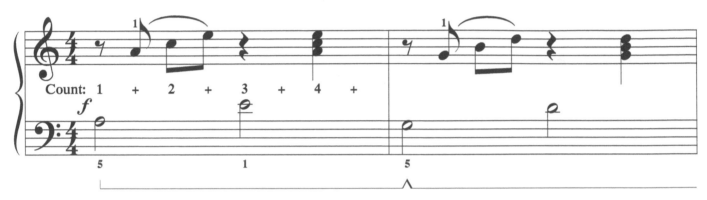

Write the chord letter name for each example (Am, E, G, etc.).

____   ____   ____   ____   ____

SIGHTREADING

DAY 2: Fiesta España

Key of _____ Major/Minor

Scan the music for a pattern. Then silently finger the L.H. chords.
Count the opening measure before sightreading.

DAY 3: Fiesta España

Key of _____ Major/Minor
(for L.H. alone)

Scan the music and notice the pattern.

DAY 4: Fiesta España

Key of _____ Major/Minor

Notice the L.H. opens with the interval of a 5th that is played with fingers 4 and 1.
Silently finger the R.H. crossover from measures 7-8.

Draw an X through the incorrect measures in 4/4. Hint: There are two.

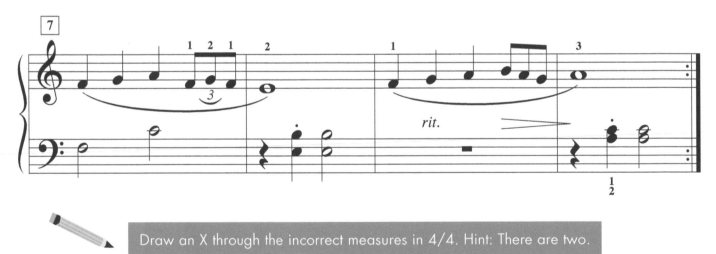

DAY 5: Fiesta España

Key of _____ Major/Minor

Scan the music and notice the patterns.
Silently finger the scale at measure 4 before sightreading.

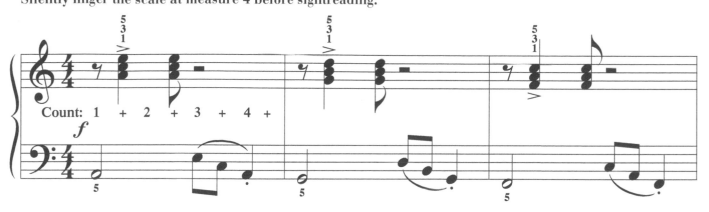

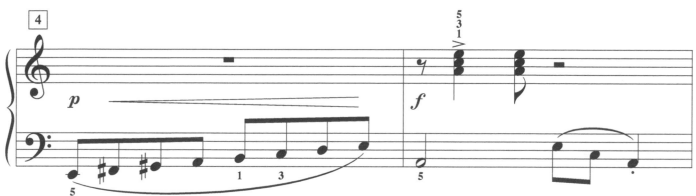

DAY 1: Sea Chantey

Key of _____ Major/Minor

Identify the two L.H. chords that are used.
Silently finger the R.H. shift from measures 5-6.

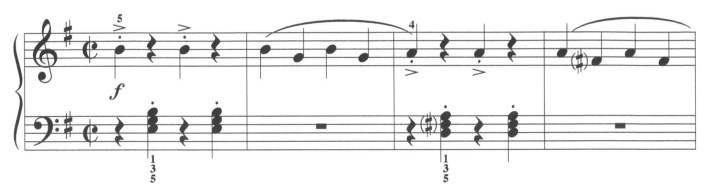

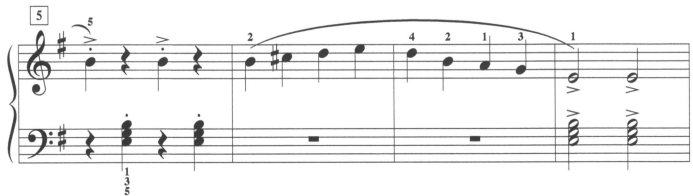

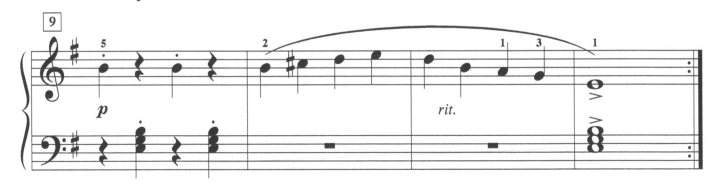

Name the major and minor key for each key signature below.

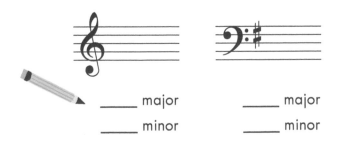

_____ major   _____ major
_____ minor   _____ minor

DAY 2: Sea Chantey

Key of _____ Major/Minor

Notice the time signature! Identify the two R.H. chords that are used and silently finger them.
Identify the two L.H. chords in the last line and finger them also.

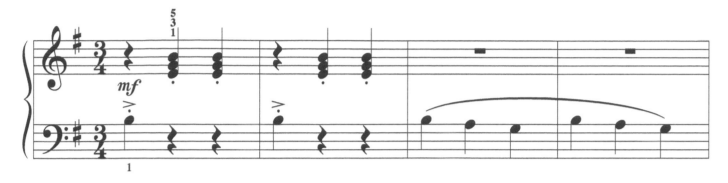

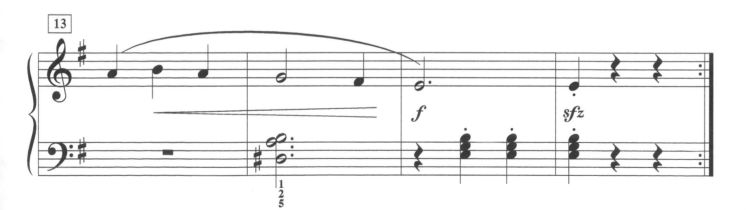

DAY 3: Sea Chantey

Key of _____ Major/Minor

Notice the key signature and the time signature.
Identify the two L.H. chords that are used. Silently finger them before sightreading.

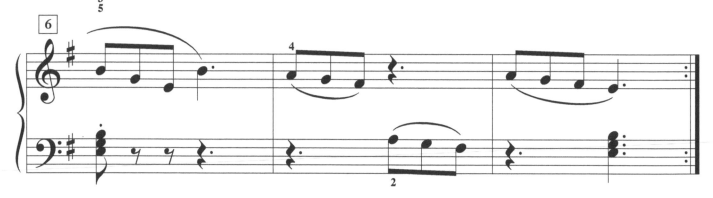

Draw bar lines for this 6/8 rhythm.
Can you tap, counting 1 2 3 4 5 6?

DAY 4: Sea Chantey

Key of _____ Major/Minor

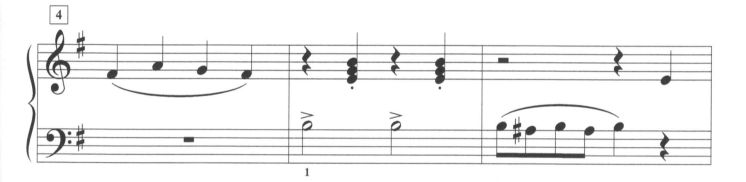

DAY 5: Sea Chantey

Key of _____ Major/Minor

Scan the music. Identify the two L.H. chords used. Silently finger them before sightreading. Notice the dynamics for the Theme and each Variation.

Theme

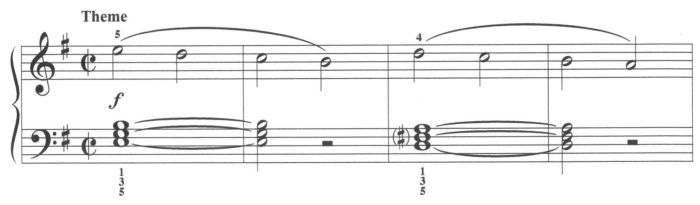

SIGHTREADING

In what octave does the L.H. begin? Notice the use of pedal in this variation.

Variation 2

Circle the example that is NOT a sequence of the motive.

motive

DAY 1: Rage Over a Lost Penny

Key of _____ Major/Minor

Scan the music. Silently finger the two L.H. chords that are used.

Draw one rest to complete each measure.

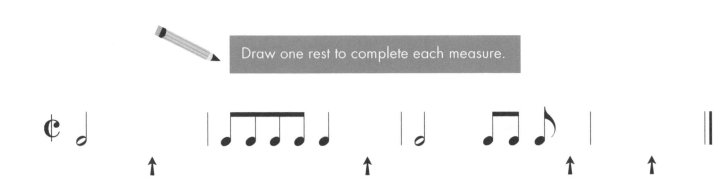

SIGHTREADING

DAY 2: Rage Over a Lost Penny

Key of _____ Major/Minor

DON'T PRACTICE THIS!

Silently finger the two R.H. chords. Remember the F♯ in the V7 chord!

Draw one note to complete each measure.

DAY 3: Rage Over a Lost Penny

Key of _____ Major/Minor

What sharp does the R.H. play in the first measure?
Silently finger the two L.H. chords before sightreading.

DAY 4: Rage Over a Lost Penny

Key of _____ Major/Minor

DAY 5: Rage Over a Lost Penny

Key of _____ Major/Minor

Notice the time signature! Silently finger the scale
in measures 13-15 before sightreading.

DAY 1: Finale
Key of _____ Major/Minor

DON'T PRACTICE THIS!

Silently finger the L.H. chords before playing. The chord symbols will guide you.

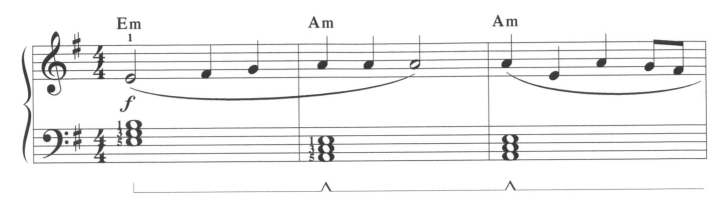

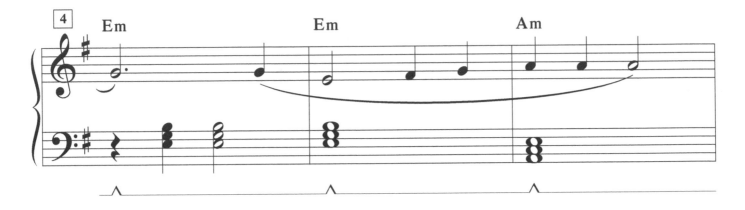

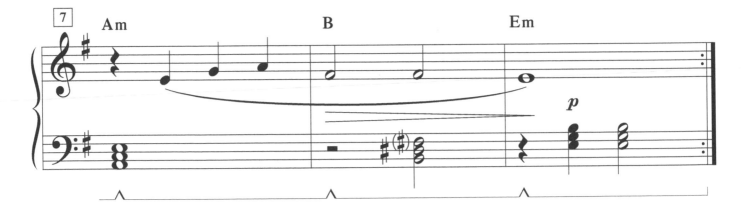

Unscramble this topsy-turvy chord.

F♯ B D♯ = _____ major

DAY 2: Finale

Key of _____ Major/Minor

Silently finger the L.H. chords before playing. The chord symbols will guide you.

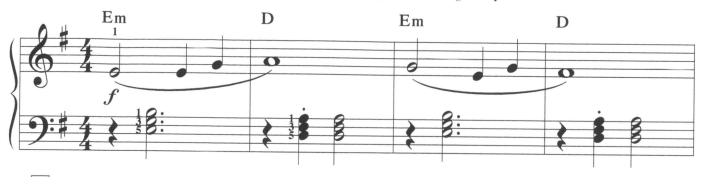

DAY 3: Finale

Key of _____ Major/Minor

Silently finger the L.H. chords before playing. Notice the dynamics.

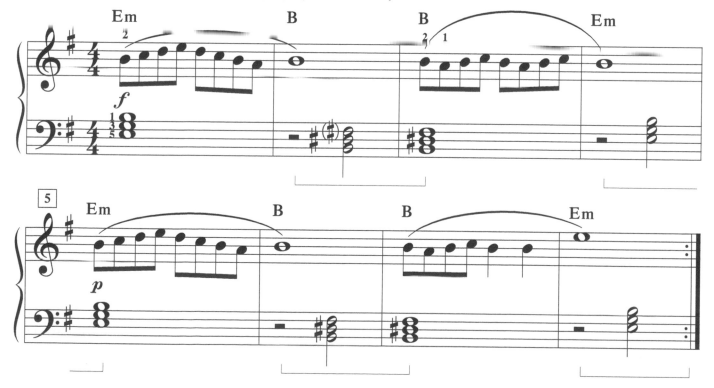

DAY 4: Finale

Key of _____ Major/Minor

Silently finger the L.H. chords before playing.

DON'T
PRACTICE
THIS!

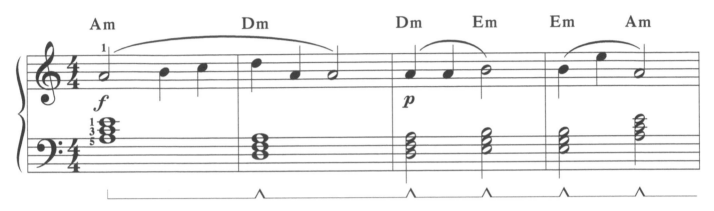

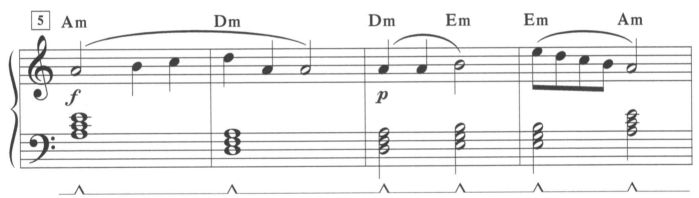

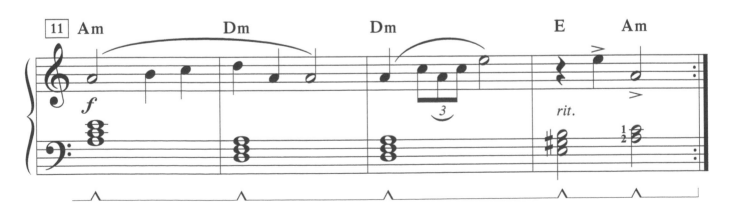

SIGHTREADING

DON'T PRACTICE THIS!

DAY 5: Finale

Key of _____ Major/Minor

Silently finger the L.H. chords before playing.
The chord symbols will guide you.

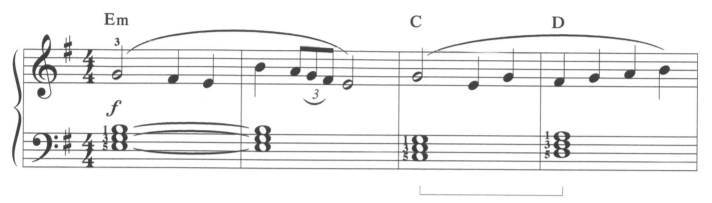

Write triplets to complete each measure.

DAY 1: Baroque Dance

Key of _____ Major/Minor

DON'T PRACTICE THIS!

Silently finger the R.H. notes in measures 1-2.

DAY 2: Baroque Dance

Key of _____ Major/Minor

(for L.H. alone)

Notice the octave in measure 1.

DAY 3: Baroque Dance

Key of _____ Major/Minor

Name each interval (2nd, 3rd, 4th, 5th, 6th, 7th, 8ve).

_____   _____   _____   _____   _____

DAY 4: Baroque Dance

Key of _____ Major/Minor

Notice the *f*–*p* echoes throughout the piece.

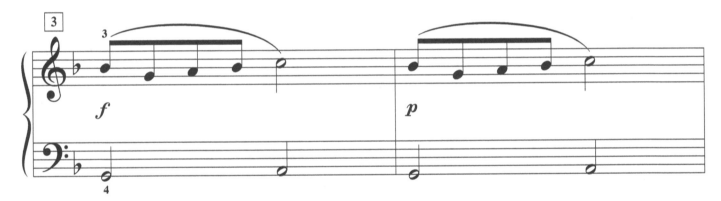

SIGHTREADING

DAY 5: Baroque Dance

Key of _____ Major/Minor

DON'T PRACTICE THIS!

Be on the alert for L.H. B♮s.

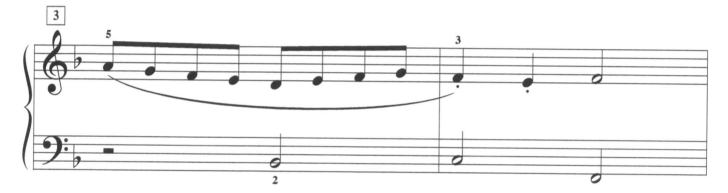

DAY 1: Legend of Madrid

Key of _____ Major/Minor

DON'T PRACTICE THIS!

Identify each L.H. broken chord as i, iv, or V7 before playing.
Which chord uses a B♭?

DAY 2: Legend of Madrid

Notice the cadenza-like passage starting at measure 5.
Silently finger measures 1–2 before playing.

SIGHTREADING

DAY 3: Legend of Madrid

Key of _____ Major / Minor

Identify each L.H. broken chord as i, iv, or V7 before playing.

DON'T PRACTICE THIS!

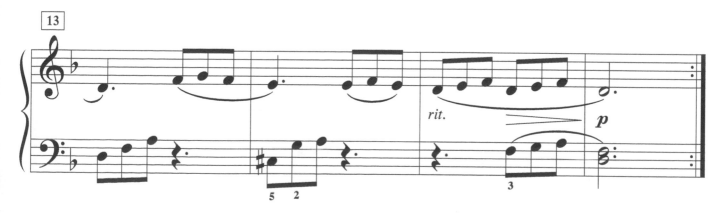

DAY 4: Legend of Madrid

Key of _____ Major/Minor

Identify each L.H. broken chord from measures 1–7
before playing (C major, D minor, etc.).

DAY 5: Legend of Madrid

Key of _____ Major/Minor

Notice the scale fingerings. Shape the music with each crescendo and diminuendo.

DAY 1: Phantom of the Keys

Key of _____ Major/Minor

DON'T PRACTICE **THIS!**

What two primary chords does the L.H. play? (i, iv, or V7)
Plan how your R.H. will play the grace note in the last measure.

Identify each minor scale as natural or harmonic.

DAY 2: Phantom of the Keys

Key of _____ Major/Minor

Plan how you will play the L.H. grace note in the opening measure.

DAY 3: Phantom of the Keys

Key of _____ Major/Minor

Notice the key signature!

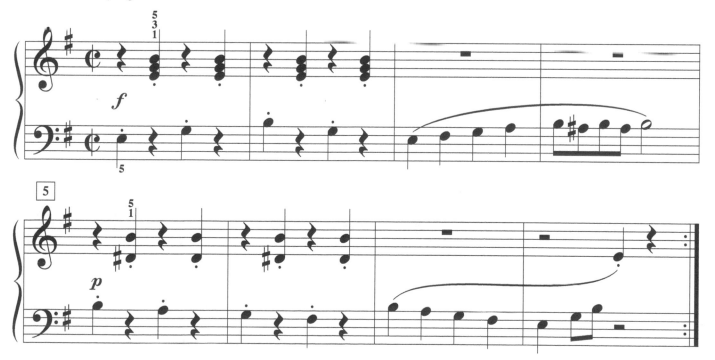

DAY 4: Phantom of the Keys

Key of _____ Major/Minor

Plan how you will play the R.H. grace note at measure 8.

SIGHTREADING

DAY 5: Phantom of the Keys

Key of _____ Major/Minor

DON'T PRACTICE THIS!

Plan how you will play the R.H. octaves and chromatic scales.

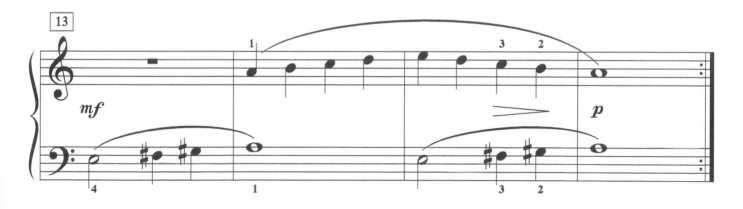

DAY 1: Humoresque

Key of _____ Major/Minor

hu**mischief** **Ostinato** **re** **Sforzando** **que**

DON'T PRACTICE THIS!

Silently finger the opening L.H. ostinato pattern before playing.
Notice the octave interval.

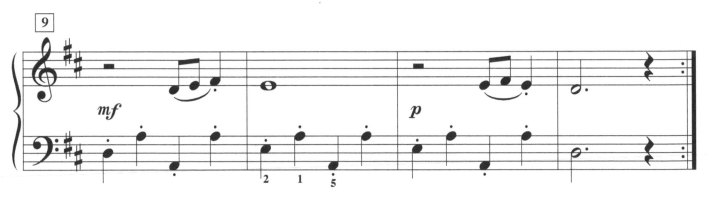

Circle the scale degree that is missing from this melody.

scale degree   1   2   3   4   5   6   7   8

DAY 2: Humoresque

Key of _____ Major/Minor

Where does the music change to minor? Where does it change back to major?

DAY 3: Humoresque

Key of _____ Major/Minor

DON'T PRACTICE THIS!

Prepare the opening octaves for each hand before playing. Scan the music carefully for the accidentals. Where will you play a chromatic passage?

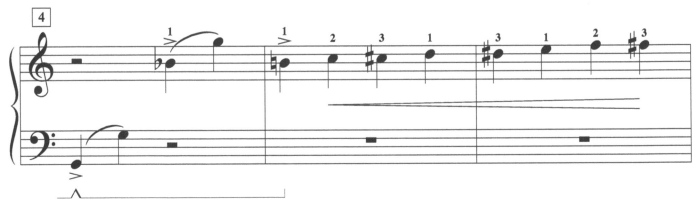

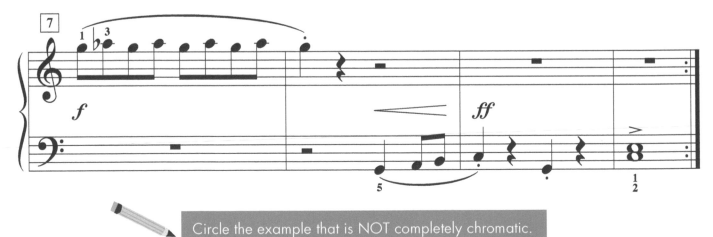

Circle the example that is NOT completely chromatic.

SIGHTREADING

DAY 4: Humoresque

Key of _____ Major/Minor

Silently finger the opening L.H. ostinato pattern before playing.

DON'T PRACTICE THIS!

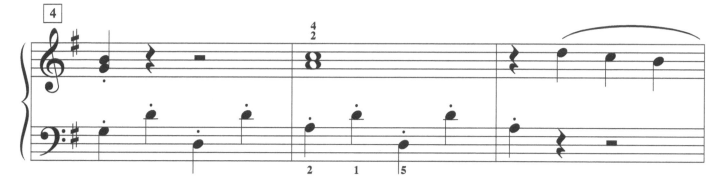

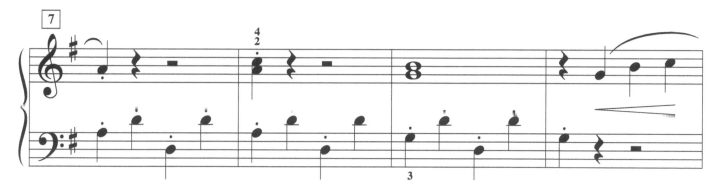

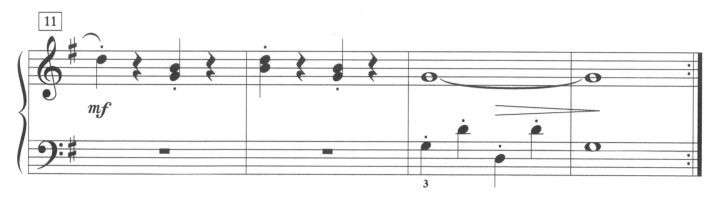

DAY 5: Humoresque

Key of _____ Major/Minor

Silently finger the opening L.H. ostinato pattern before playing.

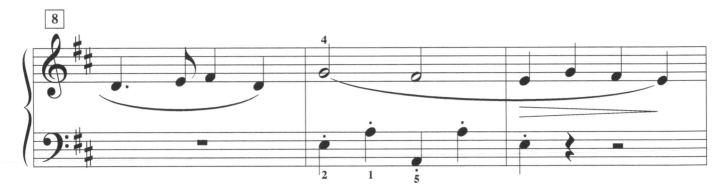

SIGHTREADING

Tap this two-handed rhythm while counting aloud: 1 + 2 + 3 + 4 +

DAY 1: The Bear

DON'T
PRACTICE
THIS!

Name the notes for the opening octave.
Where is it located on the keyboard?
Do the L.H. notes ever change?

How many measures use the interval of a 4th?
1   2   3   or   4   (circle)

DAY 2: The Bear

Does the L.H. octave ever change?
Silently finger the R.H. 3rds at measures 5-6.

DAY 3: The Bear

Notice the R.H. is written in the bass clef.

DON'T PRACTICE THIS!

DAY 4: The Bear

Does the L.H. octave ever change?

DAY 5: The Bear

Name the notes for the opening octave. Where is it located on the keyboard?
Notice the R.H. is written in the bass clef.

SIGHTREADING

DAY 1: Liebestraum

Key of _____ Major/Minor

Franz Liszt

DON'T PRACTICE THIS!

Scan the music for the L.H. broken triads.
Silently finger each.

Draw an X through the incorrect measure in 6/4.

50

DAY 2: Liebestraum

Key of _____ Major/Minor

Plan how you will play the last arpeggiated chord before playing.

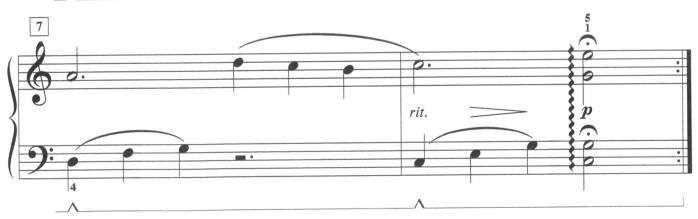

DAY 3: Liebestraum

Key of _____ Major/Minor

Silently finger the opening L.H. pattern. Notice the hands shift at measure 3.
Plan how you will play the last arpeggiated chord.

cross over

Name the major or minor chord for each example.

DAY 4: Liebestraum

Key of _____ Major/Minor

Mentally hear the rhythm of measure 1 before playing.

DAY 5: Liebestraum

Key of _____ Major/Minor

Silently finger the L.H. accompaniment pattern for measures 1–4 before playing.

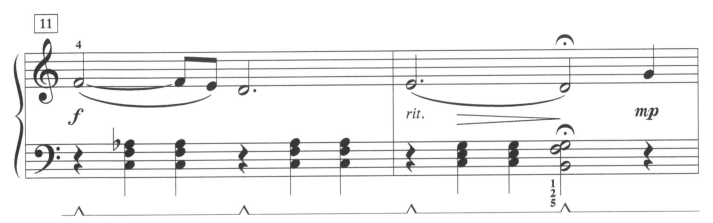

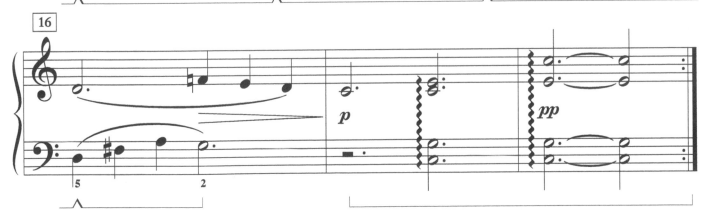

DAY 1: Barrelhouse Blues

Key of _____ Major/Minor

Scan the music. Notice the two-measure L.H. blues pattern.
The Roman numerals show the 12-bar-blues progression.

DON'T
PRACTICE
THIS!

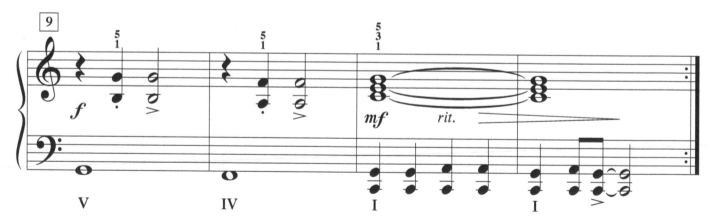

Complete the 12-bar blues chord progression by filling in the blanks: I, IV, or V

‖: I | I | ___ | I | ___ | IV | I | I | ___ | ___ | I | I :‖

DAY 2: Barrelhouse Blues

Key of _____ Major / Minor

Mentally hear the L.H. rhythm for measures 1–2 before playing.

DAY 3: Barrelhouse Blues

Key of _____ Major/Minor

Mentally hear the R.H. pattern in swing rhythm before playing.

Swing-in' the blues,___ *etc.*

DAY 4: Barrelhouse Blues

Key of _____ Major/Minor

Mentally hear the R.H. pattern in swing rhythm before playing (measure 2).

f-p on repeat

Swing-in' to the rhy-thm!

DAY 5: Barrelhouse Blues

Key of _____ Major/Minor

Scan the music. Notice the two-measure L.H. pattern. Can you write Roman numerals under the bass staff to show the 12-bar-blues progression?

Complete the 12-bar blues chord progression by filling in the blanks: I, IV, or V

‖: I | ___ | ___ | ___ ___ | ___ | I | I | ___ | ___ | I | I :‖

DAY 1: The Piano Playin' Chocolate...

Key of _____ Major/Minor

Silently finger the 6ths for the R.H. in measures 1-2.

Plan how you will play the tremolo in the last measure, including preparing the pedal.

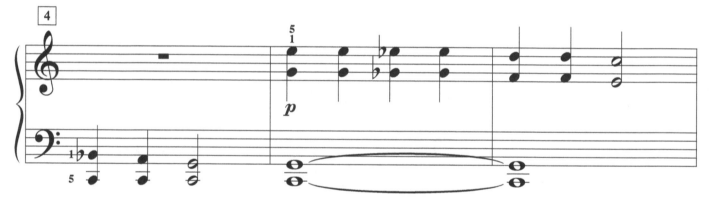

Write a 6th up or down from these notes.

SIGHTREADING

DAY 2: The Piano Playin' Chocolate…

Key of _____ Major/Minor

Silently finger the L.H. blues pattern for measures 1–2.

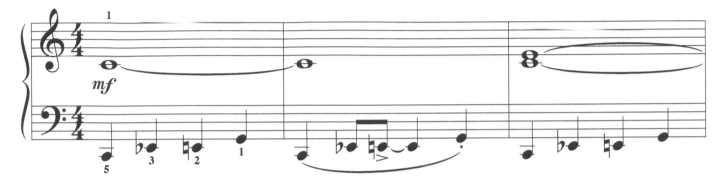

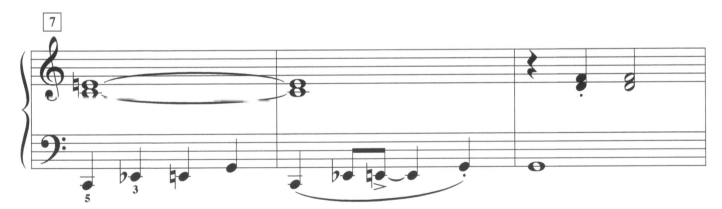

swing the 8ths!

DAY 3: The Piano Playin' Chocolate...

Key of _____ Major/Minor

DON'T PRACTICE THIS!

Silently finger the walking bass for measures 1–2.

DAY 4: The Piano Playin' Chocolate Eater's Blues

Key of _____ Major/Minor

Plan how you will play measures 1–2. Swing the 8th notes!

Lis - ten to the beat of the blues.

DAY 5: The Piano Playin' Chocolate…

Key of _____ Major/Minor

Notice the use of pedal. Be sure to hold the whole notes for four full beats!

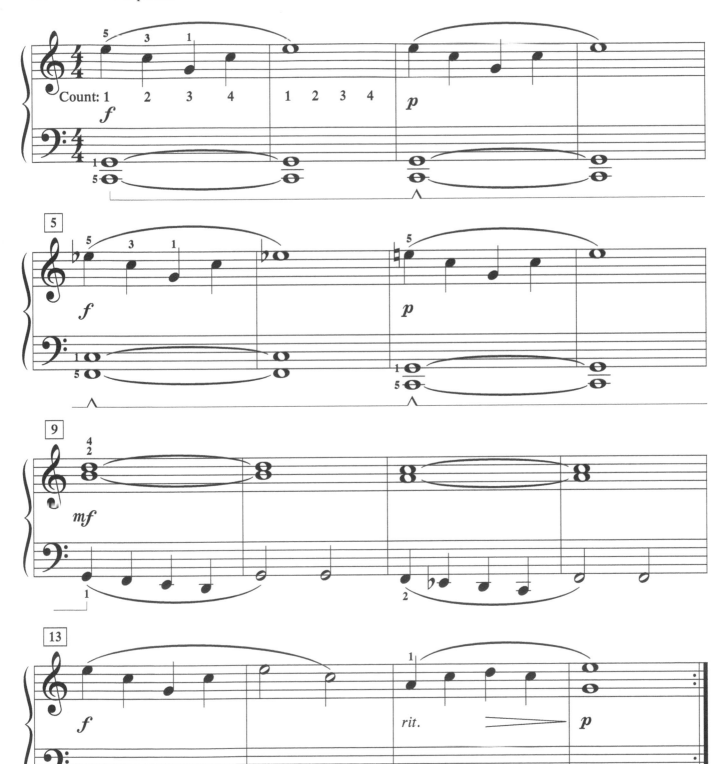

DAY 1: Gavotte

Key of _____ Major/Minor

Scan the music. Where does the R.H. play root position chords? 1st inversion chords? 2nd inversion chords?

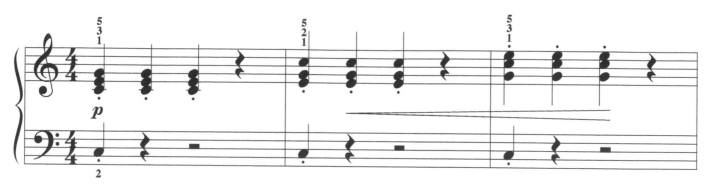

root	root	root	root	root
1st inv.	1st inv.	1st inv.	1st inv.	1st inv.
2nd inv.	2nd inv.	2nd inv.	2nd inv.	2nd inv.

DAY 2: Gavotte

Key of _____ Major/Minor

DAY 3: Gavotte

Key of _____ Major/Minor

DAY 4: Gavotte

Key of _____ Major/Minor

On what inversion does the R.H. begin?

DAY 5: Gavotte

Key of _____ Major/Minor

Plan how you will play the chords for each hand in measures 9–12.

DON'T PRACTICE THIS!

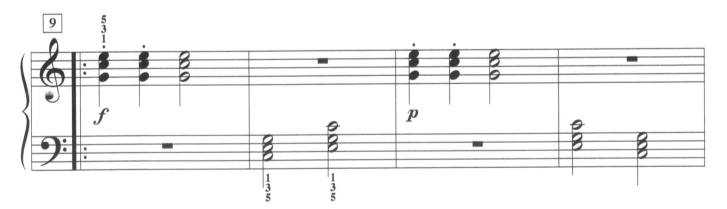

DAY 1: The Return

Key of _____ Major/Minor

Silently finger the opening broken chords.

Draw bar lines for this 6/8 rhythm.

DAY 2: The Return

Key of _____ Major/Minor

Silently finger the R.H. broken chords for measures 1–3.
Notice the use of pedal.

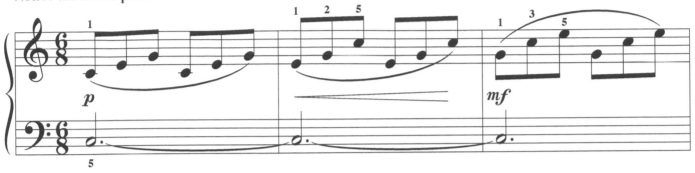

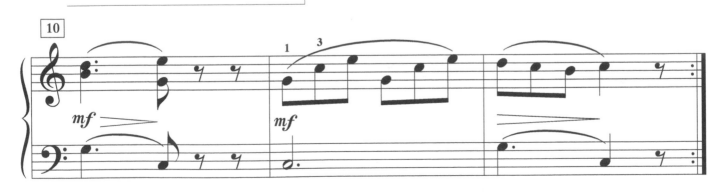

DAY 3: The Return

Key of _____ Major/Minor

DAY 4: The Return

Key of _____ Major/Minor

DAY 5: The Return

Key of _____ Major/Minor

Silently finger the R.H. for measures 1-4 before playing.

DAY 1: Swing Low, Sweet Chariot
Key of _____ Major/Minor

DON'T PRACTICE THIS!

Swing the 8th notes at measure 3.
At measure 4, remember to play the R.H. F♯.

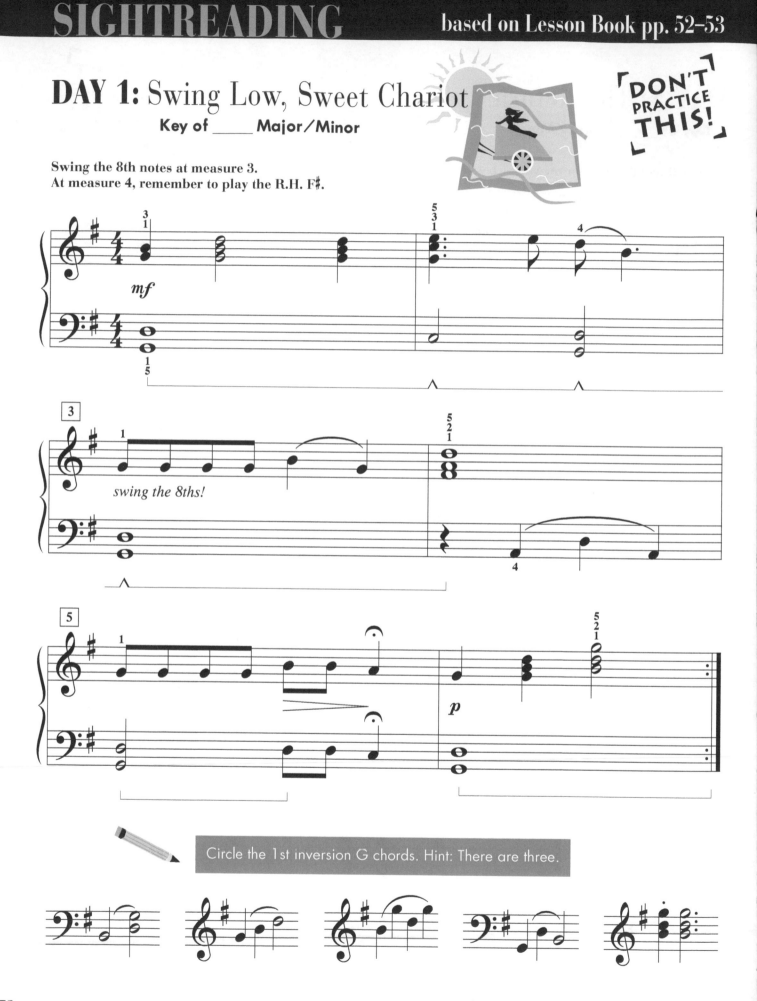

swing the 8ths!

Circle the 1st inversion G chords. Hint: There are three.

SIGHTREADING

DAY 2: Swing Low, Sweet Chariot

Key of _____ Major/Minor

Mentally hear the rhythm of measures 1-2 before playing.

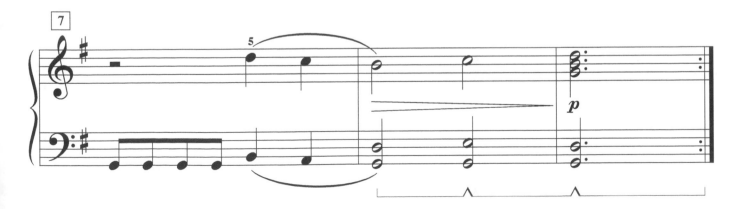

DAY 3: Swing Low, Sweet Chariot

Key of _____ Major/Minor
(for L.H. alone)

Notice the key change. Swing the 8ths at measure 3. Prepare the pedal before playing.

DAY 4: Swing Low, Sweet Chariot

Key of _____ Major/Minor

Notice the time signature has changed.

SIGHTREADING

DAY 5: Swing Low, Sweet Chariot

Key of _____ Major/Minor

Silently finger the L.H. chords for measures 1–4. Where does the L.H. play an F#?

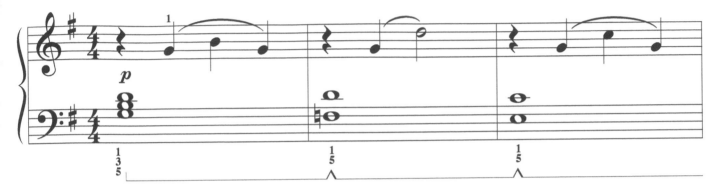

DAY 1: Rhythm Puzzle

Key of _____ Major/Minor

Scan the music. What 16th-note pattern is used throughout?

Draw bar lines for this rhythm with 16th notes.

SIGHTREADING

DAY 2: Rhythm Puzzle

Key of _____ Major/Minor

DAY 3: Rhythm Puzzle

Key of _____ Major/Minor

Mentally hear the rhythm in measure 1 before playing.
Silently finger the two L.H. chords.

DAY 4: Rhythm Puzzle

Key of _____ Major/Minor

DAY 5: Rhythm Puzzle

Key of _____ Major/Minor

DAY 1: Adagio and Allegro

Key of _____ Major/Minor

Hint: Play slowly with big tone. Notice the use of pedal.

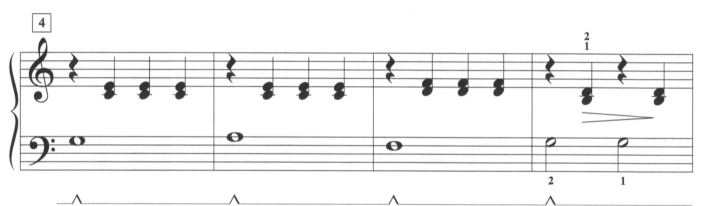

Draw an X through the incorrect measures in 4/4. Hint: There are two.

80

SIGHTREADING

DAY 2: Adagio and Allegro

Key of _____ Major/Minor

Notice the L.H. begins in the treble clef.
Silently finger the descending pattern with each hand for lines 1 and 2.

DAY 3: Adagio and Allegro

Key of _____ Major/Minor

Be on the lookout for scale fingerings!
Can you include all the dynamics?

Write two measures of your own rhythm using 16th notes.

4/4 | ‖

DAY 4: Adagio and Allegro

Key of _____ Major/Minor

Silently finger the notes with both hands for measures 1–2 before playing.

DAY 5: Adagio and Allegro

Key of _____ Major/Minor

Play slowly with big tone. Be alert for the L.H. octaves.

pedal optional

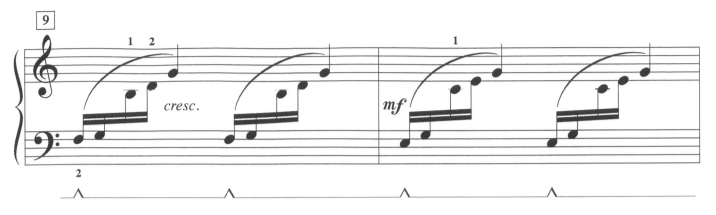

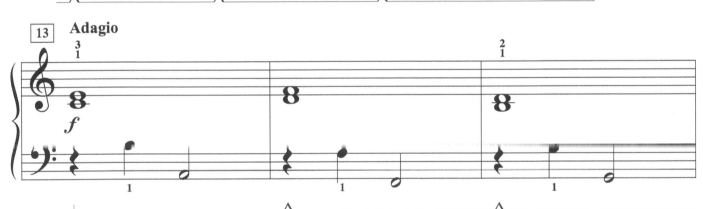

DAY 1: Gypsy Camp
Key of _____ Major/Minor

Plan how you will play the rhythm in measures 1–2 with the grace notes.

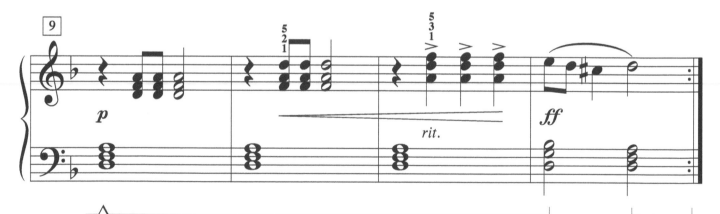

There are seven measures that use only the D minor chord. Put a ✓ above each measure.

DAY 2: Gypsy Camp

Key of _____ Major/Minor

Keep the opening L.H. 8th notes very steady!

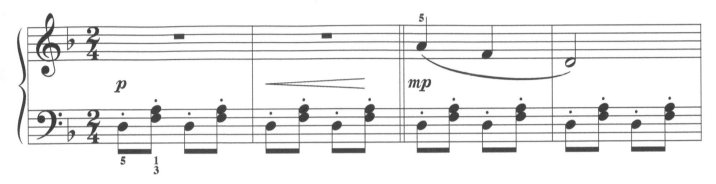

DAY 3: Gypsy Camp

Key of _____ Major/Minor

DON'T PRACTICE THIS!

What form of the minor scale is used in this piece?

DAY 4: Gypsy Camp

Key of _____ Major/Minor

Plan how you will play the rhythm in measures 1–2 with the grace notes.

DAY 5: Gypsy Camp

Key of _____ Major/Minor

Silently finger the opening measures. Do you see the pattern?
Notice measure 12 has a *molto rit.* with a fermata.

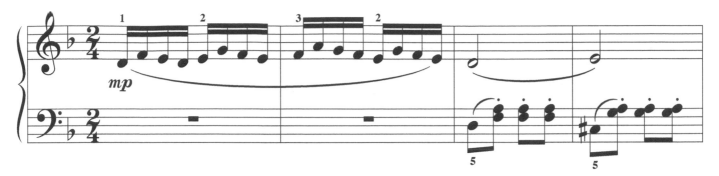

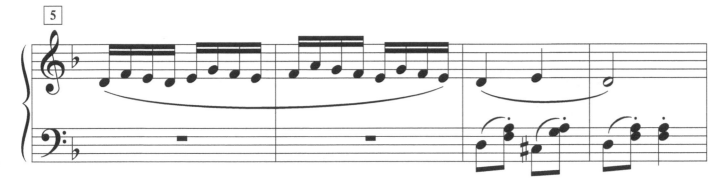

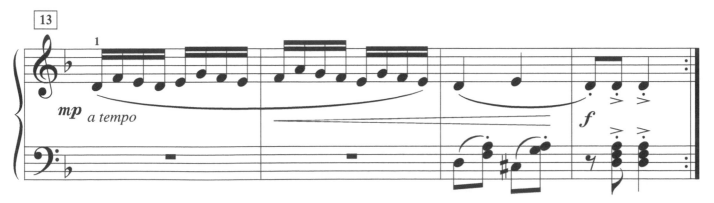

DAY 1: Pachelbel Canon

DON'T PRACTICE THIS!

The chord symbols will help alert you to changing harmonies and hand shifts.

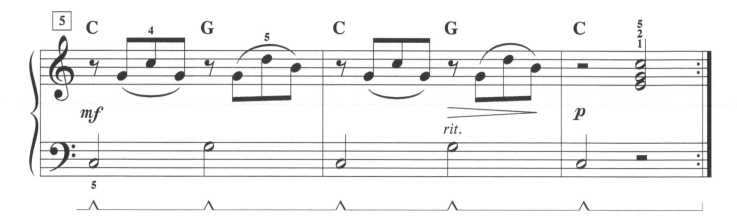

The L.H. plays only the roots of the chords. True or False? (circle)

DAY 2: Pachelbel Canon

DON'T PRACTICE THIS!

Scan the music and notice the hand shifts.
Mentally hear the rhythm of measure 5 before playing.

DAY 3: Pachelbel Canon

Set a slow, steady beat and watch for 16th-note rhythm patterns.

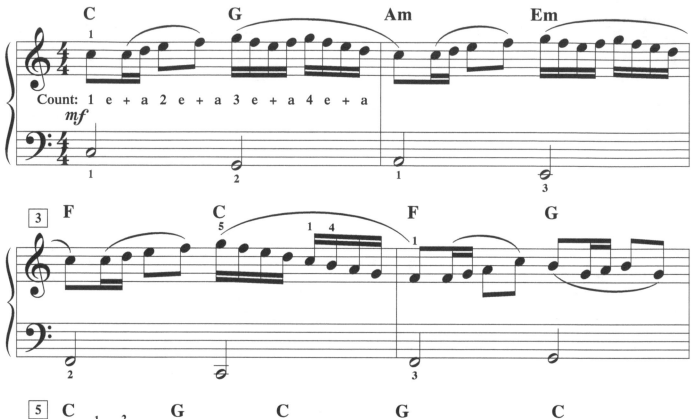

Count: 1 e + a 2 e + a 3 e + a 4 e + a

Complete each measure with one or more 16th-note patterns:

DAY 4: Pachelbel Canon

(for L.H. alone)

This melody uses a pattern and sequence.
Scan the music noticing the hand shift for each measure.

DON'T
PRACTICE
THIS!

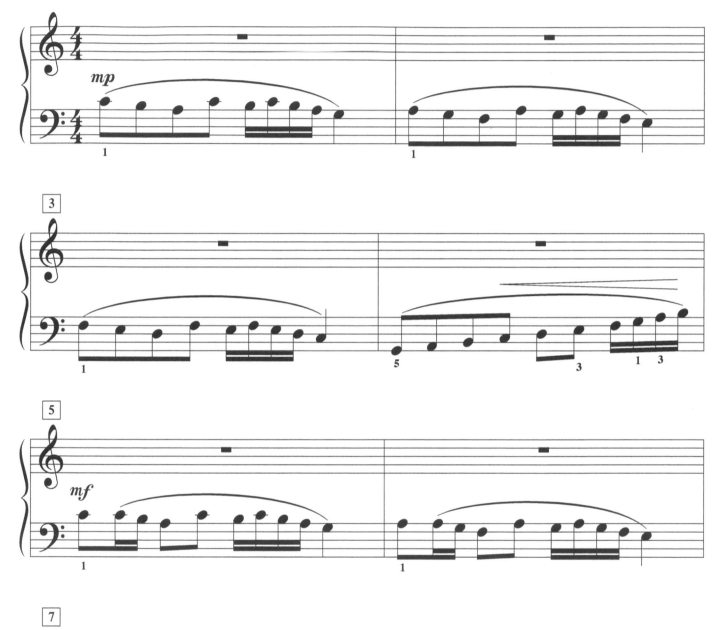

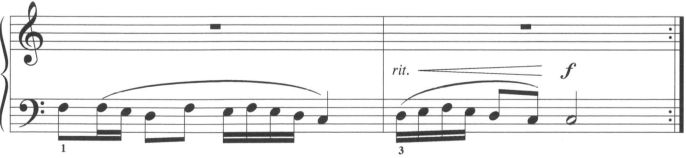

DAY 5: Pachelbel Canon

DON'T PRACTICE THIS!

Scan the music thinking through the rhythm.
Some counting is shown to guide you.

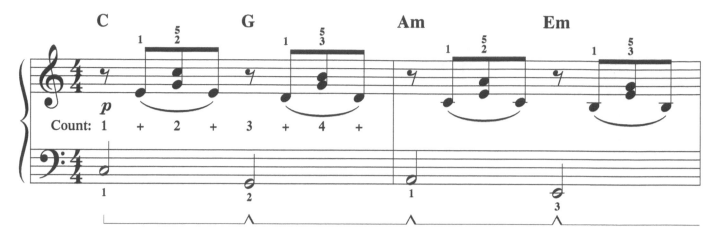

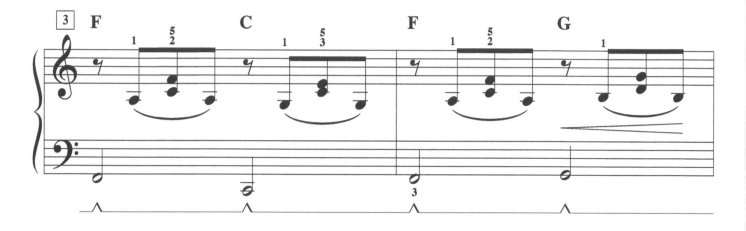

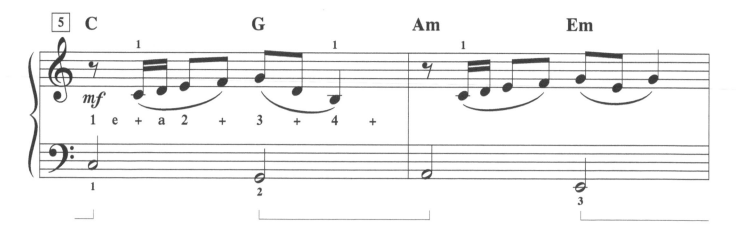

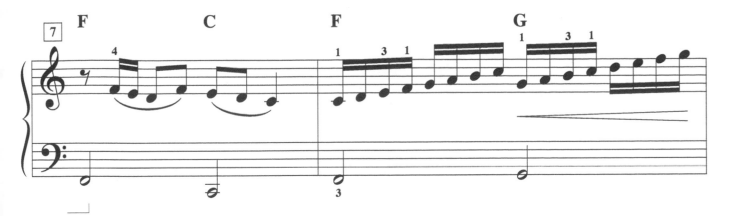

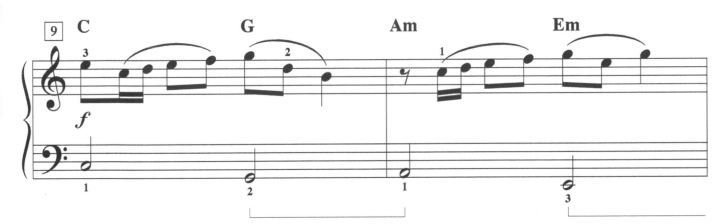

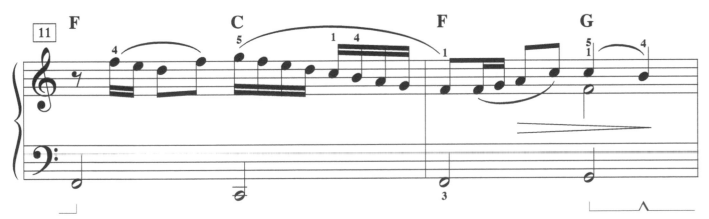

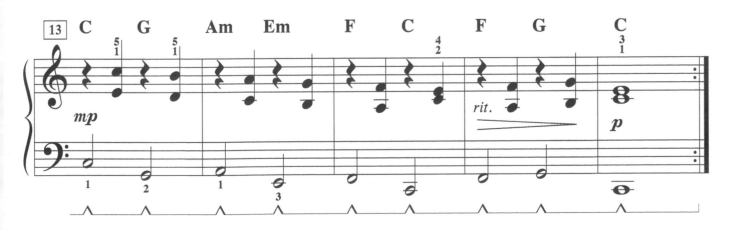

Piano Adventures® Certificate
CONGRATULATIONS

_____

(Your Name)

You are now a Level 3B Sightreader.
Keep up the great work!

_____

Teacher

_____

Date

V102022